THE CRYPTO CANVAS: PAINTING THE FUTURE WITH BLOCKCHAIN

JUANCA ROJAS

DEDICATION

I dedicate this first project to my family, friends, and each person who has been part of my life from before my birth until the publication of this book. It is thanks to them that I was shaped to reach this wonderful point in my life.

Table of Contents

Introduction

Welcome to an exciting journey through blockchain technology and its impact on economic and business fields. In a constantly changing world, technological innovation is the driving force behind transformation in all aspects of our lives, and blockchain has emerged as one of the most revolutionary innovations of the digital era.

This book is a comprehensive guide that explores the multiple facets of blockchain technology and how it is reshaping the economic and business landscape. As we progress on this journey, we will discover how blockchain has transcended the bounds of cryptocurrency to influence a variety of industries, from finance to healthcare, from logistics to energy, and beyond.

Within these pages, you will find a detailed exploration of how blockchain is enhancing security, transparency, and efficiency across various sectors. You will learn how blockchain technology is fueling a revolution in data and asset management, offering solutions to the most pressing challenges of our time.

From smart contracts automating business processes to digital identity management and supply chain traceability, you will see how blockchain is redefining how we conduct business and manage resources. Through practical examples and case studies, you will gain a deeper understanding of how this technology is transforming the global economy.

As we progress on this journey, it is important to recognize that while blockchain offers innovative solutions, it also poses challenges and questions that must be addressed as its adoption expands. From privacy and security issues to regulatory and interoperability challenges, this book will guide you through the key considerations that must be addressed as blockchain continues to evolve.

I hope this book inspires you to explore and harness the potential of blockchain technology in your field of interest. Whether you are a finance professional, a healthcare professional, a content creator, an entrepreneur, or a sustainability enthusiast, you will find that blockchain offers exciting and transformative opportunities.

Blockchain technology is a beacon on the horizon of innovation, and this book will help you navigate its ever-changing waters. May this journey inspire you to explore new frontiers and be part of the blockchain revolution that is redefining our economic and business world!

Juan Camilo Rojas   November 1, 2023

Chapter 1: The Fundamentals of Blockchain Technology

Introduction

In the world of technology, advancements come and go, but rarely does an innovation emerge that radically changes the way we live, work, and conduct business. Blockchain technology is one such disruptive innovation that is on its way to redefine our perception of security, trust, and efficiency in the digital environment. In the current era of global interconnectedness, the need for a reliable infrastructure to support our transactions, data, and digital assets has become more crucial than ever. It is in this context that blockchain technology has emerged as a beacon of innovation, capable of illuminating the path toward a safer and more efficient digital future.

This introductory chapter aims to demystify blockchain technology, explore its fundamentals, and provide a solid foundation for understanding how it is transforming various industries. We will address key questions such as: What is blockchain technology? How does it work? Why is it so important and relevant in today's world? What are the essential characteristics that define it and make it unique?

Functioning of Blockchain Technology

At the core of blockchain technology is an innovative way of recording data. Imagine an endless chain of blocks, where each block contains specific information. What makes this chain special is its decentralized and secure structure. Instead of relying on a centralized server, data in a blockchain is stored in a distributed network of nodes. This means that there is no single entity with control over the information and transactions; rather, it depends on a network of participants.

Each block in the blockchain contains a set of transactions and a unique digital signature that links it to the previous block. This ensures that blocks are immutable, meaning that once a transaction is recorded in a block, it cannot be modified or deleted without the consensus of the majority of participants in the network. This immutability feature is fundamental to the trust and integrity of data in blockchain technology.

Key Features

The key features of blockchain technology are what make it so powerful and transformative in a variety of fields:

1. **Decentralization:** Unlike traditional centralized systems, where a central entity has control over information and transactions, blockchain operates on a decentralized network of nodes. This decentralization eliminates single points of failure and avoids dependence on intermediaries.

2. **Security:** Security is a fundamental principle in blockchain. Cryptography ensures that data stored on the blockchain is highly secure. Digital signature technology protects transactions and data integrity, making it extremely difficult to alter them without detection.

3. **Transparency:** All transactions on the blockchain are transparent and visible to all participants in the network. This transparency promotes trust and integrity in a transactional environment.

4. **Immutability:** Once a transaction is recorded on the blockchain, it becomes part of an immutable historical record. This is essential to ensure data integrity and transaction traceability.

In the upcoming chapters, we will explore how these features translate into a series of applications across a wide range of economic and business fields. From the impact of cryptocurrencies on the global economy to the transformation of supply chains and identity management, blockchain has become a versatile and valuable tool for addressing contemporary world challenges.

As we progress through this book, we invite you to embark on a journey of discovery. We will explore how blockchain technology is revolutionizing the way we live and work in the digital era. Beyond being a futuristic promise, blockchain technology is a reality that is already transforming how we conduct business and manage information. We stand on the threshold of a new digital paradigm, and this book will serve as a guide on this exciting exploration of the infinite possibilities that blockchain technology offers.

Chapter 2: Cryptocurrencies and Decentralized Finance (DeFi)

Bitcoin and the Rise of Cryptocurrencies

At the dawn of the 21st century, a groundbreaking event in the world of digital finance transformed the perception of money and how people interact with it. The emergence of Bitcoin in 2009, driven by the pseudonym Satoshi Nakamoto, marked the birth of cryptocurrencies. Bitcoin, often referred to as "digital gold," is a decentralized digital currency that enables individuals to transact and store value without the need for traditional intermediaries such as banks and governments.

The significance of Bitcoin lies in its ability to address some of the fundamental issues that have persisted in conventional finance. It offers a global payment system that operates 24/7, with minimal transaction fees and without the geographic restrictions characteristic of traditional currencies. Furthermore, Bitcoin's limited supply (21 million) makes it a deflationary asset, meaning its value tends to increase over time rather than decrease due to inflation.

Decentralized Finance (DeFi)

The emergence of Bitcoin paved the way for a new financial paradigm: decentralized finance, or DeFi. DeFi represents a financial ecosystem that operates autonomously on a blockchain network, without the need for intermediaries such as banks, brokers, or traditional financial institutions. It is based on the philosophy that all individuals should have access to secure, transparent, and accessible financial services regardless of their geographical location or economic status.

DeFi applications range from lending and borrowing to asset exchange, staking, and yield generation. The cryptocurrency Ether (ETH) and the Ethereum network have been instrumental in the expansion of DeFi, providing the necessary infrastructure for the creation of smart contracts, which are computer programs that automate and execute financial agreements.

The DeFi Ecosystem

The DeFi ecosystem consists of a wide variety of projects and protocols, each designed to address specific aspects of decentralized finance. Some notable examples include:

- **Loan and Borrowing Protocols:** Platforms like Aave, Compound, and MakerDAO allow users to lend and borrow digital assets, using cryptocurrencies as collateral to secure loans without the need for a traditional bank.

- **Decentralized Exchanges (DEXs):** Uniswap and SushiSwap are examples of DEXs that enable users to exchange cryptocurrencies without an intermediary. They use smart contracts to facilitate the trading of assets.

- **Staking and Yield:** Platforms like Yearn.Finance and Synthetix offer ways to stake cryptocurrencies to generate yields and rewards.

- **DeFi Derivatives:** Platforms like dYdX and Perpetual Protocol allow users to trade decentralized derivatives, such as futures and options, on a blockchain network.

Regulatory Challenges in DeFi

Despite its promises, DeFi is not exempt from regulatory challenges. Since transactions in DeFi are conducted anonymously and without intermediaries, questions arise about anti-money laundering prevention and compliance with financial regulations. Governments worldwide are assessing how to address this new form of finance and how to balance innovation with safety and regulation.

As we progress through this chapter and the book, we will explore in more detail how cryptocurrencies and DeFi are transforming the financial world and how they are evolving to tackle the regulatory and technical challenges they face. The decentralized finance revolution is an exciting chapter in the history of finance and technology, and we are at the epicenter of this disruptive movement that has the potential to empower individuals worldwide.

Chapter 3: Transformation of the Supply Chain and Logistics

Introduction

The supply chain and logistics are critical components of the global economy. They are responsible for transporting products and services from their origin to their final destination, involving a series of processes that include multiple stakeholders such as suppliers, manufacturers, distributors, and retailers. However, for a long time, these processes have been plagued by inefficiencies, lack of transparency, and challenges in traceability. Blockchain technology has emerged as a promising solution to address these issues and transform the way supply chains and logistics operate.

Challenges in Traditional Supply Chain and Logistics

Before exploring how blockchain is changing these fields, it is crucial to understand the inherent challenges in traditional supply chains and logistics. Some of these challenges include:

1. **Lack of Transparency:** Opacity in supply chains often makes it difficult to trace the origin of products, leading to

issues such as the spread of counterfeit products or the inability to effectively respond to quality problems.

2. **Inefficiencies and Delays:** Manual processes and fragmented communication chains can result in inefficiencies, delays, and unnecessary costs in the supply chain.

3. **Security Risks and Fraud:** The lack of security in the supply chain can lead to fraudulent activities, such as theft and product counterfeiting.

Transformation of the Supply Chain with Blockchain

Blockchain offers effective solutions to these challenges through its set of key features:

1. **Transparency:** Blockchain provides an immutable and transparent record of all transactions and events throughout the supply chain. This allows stakeholders to track the flow of products and verify their authenticity.

2. **Traceability:** The ability to trace products from their origin to their final destination is crucial in the supply chain. Thanks to the blockchain, each stage of a product's journey can be recorded, facilitating issue identification and quick action in the case of product recalls.

3. **Automation:** Smart contracts, computer programs that automatically execute when certain conditions are met, enable the automation of tasks and processes in the

supply chain. This includes payment management, alert issuance, and shipment coordination.

Examples of Blockchain Applications in the Supply Chain

Blockchain applications in the supply chain are diverse and promising. Some examples include:

- **Food Tracking:** Food companies use blockchain to trace the origin of products from the field to the consumer's table. This is essential for food safety and efficient response to disease outbreaks.
- **Asset and Logistics Management:** Blockchain technology enables real-time tracking of assets and goods in transit, reducing the risk of loss and theft. Additionally, it improves shipment coordination and reduces delays.
- **Sustainability and Labeling:** Organizations can use blockchain to verify and authenticate the origin of sustainable products, such as organic or fair-trade-certified products.
- **Waste Reduction:** Enhanced traceability and process automation in the supply chain allow more efficient resource management and waste reduction.

Challenges and Considerations

Despite the benefits that blockchain offers in the supply chain, there are challenges that must be addressed. These include interoperability between blockchain systems, widespread adoption, and ensuring data security.

With the ongoing transformation of the supply chain and logistics, blockchain is consolidating as an essential tool to improve efficiency, transparency, and security in these sectors. As we continue to explore blockchain applications in other economic and business fields, this chapter serves as a reminder of how this technology is making a difference in the way products and services reach our hands.

Chapter 4: The Transformation of Healthcare and Health Management

Introduction

Healthcare is one of the most critical pillars of any society. Ensuring access to high-quality healthcare services and efficient health management are global challenges. However, this industry has been plagued by challenges related to the interoperability of medical records, patient data security, and the lack of transparency in healthcare systems. Blockchain technology has positioned itself as a solution that can revolutionize healthcare and health management by addressing these fundamental issues.

Challenges in Traditional Healthcare

Traditional healthcare has faced a series of challenges over time:

1. **Lack of Interoperability of Medical Records:** Electronic medical records are stored in isolated systems that often cannot efficiently share information. This hinders care coordination and can lead to duplication of tests and ineffective treatments.

2. **Data Security and Privacy:** Patient data privacy is crucial, but traditional healthcare systems have experienced security breaches and data leaks that expose confidential information.

3. **Transparency in Healthcare:** Patients often lack visibility into the costs and quality of healthcare services, making informed decision-making challenging.

Transformation of Healthcare with Blockchain

Blockchain offers effective solutions to address these challenges:

1. **Interoperability of Medical Records:** Blockchain provides a decentralized platform that allows different healthcare providers and health systems to securely share medical records. Patients can grant access to their data through specific permissions, facilitating care coordination and data-driven decision-making.

2. **Data Security:** Blockchain's cryptographic technology ensures the protection of patient health data. Medical records are securely stored and can be accessed only through private keys, reducing the risk of data leaks.

3. **Transparency and Traceability:** Blockchain enables a transparent and tamper-proof record of health data, providing patients and providers with a clear view of healthcare history and associated costs. Additionally, traceability in the supply chain of medical products, such as drugs and vaccines, enhances product safety and authenticity.

Examples of Blockchain Applications in Healthcare

Blockchain applications in healthcare are diverse and promising. Some examples include:

- **Electronic Health Records:** Blockchains enable secure access and sharing of electronic health records among different health systems and providers.
- **Clinical Trial Data Management:** Blockchain improves the integrity and traceability of data in clinical trials, essential for medical research.
- **Medication Authentication:** Blockchain is used to verify the authenticity of medications and track their origin, crucial for combating counterfeiting and ensuring patient safety.
- **Donor and Organ Registry:** Blockchain technology facilitates the registration of organ donors and improves the traceability and management of transplanted organs.

Challenges and Considerations

Despite advances in applying blockchain in healthcare, significant challenges exist, such as ensuring system interoperability and overcoming regulatory and privacy barriers. Additionally, ethical and legal concerns regarding ownership and control of health data must be addressed.

The transformation of healthcare and health management through blockchain is an exciting and evolving area. As we continue to explore the applications of this technology in other fields, this chapter highlights how blockchain is enhancing healthcare by providing more transparency, security, and efficiency, ultimately translating into higher-quality healthcare and better health management.

Chapter 5: Blockchain in Identity and Security

Introduction

Identity and security are fundamental aspects of life in the digital era. From managing personal credentials to protecting confidential data, the need for robust and secure solutions is evident. Blockchain technology has emerged as a response to these challenges, offering a means to ensure the integrity of identity and data security in an increasingly interconnected world.

Challenges in Traditional Identity and Security

Identity and security have been persistent challenges in the digital world:

1. **Identity Theft:** Identity theft is a constant online threat with serious financial and personal consequences.

2. **Weak Passwords:** Passwords often serve as the sole security barrier between users and their data, making them prone to compromise.

3. **Credential Management:** Credential management and secure authentication are essential, especially in financial and governmental applications.

Blockchain for Identity and Security

Blockchain offers effective solutions to address these challenges:

1. **Decentralized Authentication:** Blockchain technology enables decentralized authentication, allowing users to access services and verify their identity without the need for a central intermediary. This reduces the risk of identity theft.

2. **Identity Management:** Users can have control over their identity and who accesses their information, enhancing privacy and security.

3. **Smart Contracts:** Smart contracts are used to establish rules for accessing information and systems, improving security in critical applications.

4. **Digital Signature:** Blockchain cryptography enables digital signatures, which are secure and ensure the authenticity of documents and transactions.

Examples of Blockchain Applications in Identity and Security

Applications of blockchain in identity and security are diverse and promising. Some examples include:

- **Sovereign Digital Identity:** Users can have a self-sovereign and verifiable digital identity on the blockchain, allowing them to control their personal information and share only what they choose.

- **Credential and Diploma Management:** Educational institutions can issue diplomas and certificates on the blockchain, reducing the risk of forgeries.
- **Cybersecurity:** Blockchain is used to enhance cybersecurity by identifying and tracking threats in real-time.
- **Authorization and Access Control:** Smart contracts on the blockchain enable precise control over access to systems and data, essential in financial and healthcare applications.

Challenges and Considerations

Despite advances in applying blockchain in identity and security, challenges exist, such as widespread adoption and the need to ensure data privacy. Additionally, legal and ethical issues related to the ownership and control of online identity must be addressed.

The transformation of identity and security through blockchain is an exciting and evolving area. As we continue to explore the applications of this technology in other fields, this chapter highlights how blockchain is improving security and identity management in a digital world, giving individuals greater control over their data and online privacy.

Chapter 6: Blockchain in Intellectual Property and Copyright

Introduction

Intellectual property (IP) and copyrights are fundamental to protecting creativity and innovation in the digital era. However, piracy and copyright infringement remain significant challenges. Blockchain technology has emerged as a solution to address these issues and ensure the integrity of intellectual property and copyrights in an ever-changing world.

Challenges in Traditional Intellectual Property and Copyright

IP and copyrights face significant challenges in the digital era:

1. **Piracy and Counterfeiting:** Unauthorized distribution of digital content and the proliferation of counterfeit products threaten copyrights and intellectual property.

2. **Complexity in Rights Management:** Copyright management often involves multiple stakeholders, leading to disputes and delays in royalty payments.

3. **Registration and Proof of Authorship:** Demonstrating authorship and original creation can be challenging in legal copyright disputes.

Blockchain for Intellectual Property and Copyright

Blockchain offers effective solutions to address these challenges:

1. **Immutable Registration:** Blockchain enables the immutable registration of creative works and copyrights. Once a work is registered, it becomes part of a historical record that cannot be modified or deleted.

2. **Proof of Authorship:** Blockchain provides a secure and verifiable way to prove the authorship of a work and its original creation. This is valuable in legal copyright disputes.

3. **Automated Rights Management:** Smart contracts on the blockchain allow for the automation of copyright and royalty management. When a licensed work is used, payments are automatically distributed to rights holders.

4. **Transparency in Content Market:** Blockchain offers a transparent platform for the content market, allowing creators and consumers to interact directly and reduce intermediaries.

Examples of Blockchain Applications in Intellectual Property and Copyright

Blockchain applications in IP and copyright are diverse and promising. Some examples include:

- **Copyright Registration:** Creators can securely register their works on the blockchain to establish proof of authorship and date.

- **Music Streaming Platforms:** Platforms like Audius use blockchain to enable artists to have greater control and receive a fairer percentage of streaming revenues.

- **Content Timestamps:** Blockchain timestamps are used to demonstrate the authorship and original creation of creative works, such as digital art and music.

- **Digital Art Sales:** Digital art is sold on blockchain markets, ensuring the authenticity and ownership of digital collectibles.

Challenges and Considerations

Despite advances in applying blockchain to IP and copyrights, challenges remain, including widespread adoption and addressing legal issues in copyright disputes. Additionally, ensuring the protection of privacy and personal data in these applications is essential.

The transformation of intellectual property and copyrights through blockchain is an exciting area promising increased protection and control for creators and rights holders. As we continue exploring the applications of this technology in other fields, this chapter highlights how blockchain is improving the management and protection of intellectual property and copyrights in an increasingly digital and globalized world.

Chapter 7: Blockchain in the Food Supply Chain

Introduction

The food supply chain is a critical component of modern life, and ensuring the quality and safety of the food we consume is of utmost importance. However, this supply chain has faced challenges related to a lack of transparency, limited traceability, and inefficiency. Blockchain technology has emerged as a solution to address these issues and ensure the integrity and security of the food supply chain.

Challenges in Traditional Food Supply Chain

The traditional food supply chain faces several challenges:

1. **Lack of Transparency:** The lack of visibility and transparency in the supply chain makes it difficult to identify quality issues and respond effectively to foodborne disease outbreaks.

2. **Limited Traceability:** The ability to trace food from its origin to the end consumer is often limited, making it

challenging to identify defective or contaminated products.

3. **Documentation and Regulatory Compliance:** The food supply chain involves a significant amount of documentation and regulatory compliance, leading to inefficiencies and errors.

Blockchain in the Food Supply Chain

Blockchain offers effective solutions to address these challenges:

1. **Transparency:** Blockchain provides a transparent and immutable record of all transactions and events in the food supply chain. This enables real-time visibility into products and their origin.

2. **Traceability:** The ability to trace food from its origin to its final destination is crucial for food safety. Blockchain records each stage of a product's journey, facilitating the identification of issues and prompt action in the event of product recalls.

3. **Automation and Smart Contracts:** Smart contracts on blockchain enable the automation of tasks and processes in the supply chain. This includes payment management, issuing alerts, and coordinating shipments.

4. **Security:** Blockchain's cryptographic technology ensures that data in the food supply chain is secure and protected against manipulation and unauthorized access.

Examples of Blockchain Applications in the Food Supply Chain

Blockchain applications in the food supply chain are diverse and promising. Some examples include:

- **Fresh Food Tracking:** Consumers can scan QR codes on food products to access detailed information about their origin and supply chain.

- **Cold Chain Management:** Blockchain is used to record and ensure that perishable foods are maintained at the appropriate temperature during transportation and storage.

- **Food Safety:** In the event of product recalls, blockchain enables the rapid identification of affected batches, minimizing risks to consumers.

- **Origin Verification:** Food products can be authenticated and verified at their origin, reducing the proliferation of counterfeit foods.

Challenges and Considerations

Despite the benefits that blockchain offers in the food supply chain, significant challenges exist, such as interoperability between blockchain systems and widespread adoption. Additionally, regulatory and privacy concerns in data management within this supply chain need to be addressed.

The transformation of the food supply chain through blockchain is an exciting and evolving area. As we continue exploring the applications of this technology in other fields, this chapter highlights how blockchain is improving security and efficiency in the food supply chain, ensuring that the food we consume is safer and more reliable.

Chapter 8: Blockchain in Energy and Sustainability

Introduction

Energy and sustainability are crucial issues in the modern world. The pursuit of sustainable energy sources and efficient management of energy resources is essential to address climate change and ensure a sustainable future. Blockchain technology has emerged as a valuable tool in the quest for solutions to these challenges by enhancing efficiency and transparency in the energy sector.

Challenges in the Traditional Energy Sector

The traditional energy sector faces several challenges:

1. **Energy Waste:** Generation and distribution of energy often result in resource wastage and significant losses.

2. **Limited Transparency:** Lack of transparency in the energy supply chain makes it difficult to identify inefficiencies and track the origin of energy.

3. **Resource Management:** Management of energy resources, such as electrical grids and energy sources, can be inefficient and unsustainable.

Blockchain in the Energy Sector and Sustainability Blockchain offers effective solutions to address these challenges:

1. **Smart Grid Management**: Blockchain is used in smart grid management to enable distributed energy generation and the sale of surplus energy to other consumers.

2. **Transparency in Energy Origin:** The blockchain provides a transparent record of energy generation and distribution, allowing consumers to verify the origin and sustainability of the energy they consume.

3. **Peer-to-Peer Energy Trading:** Smart contracts on the blockchain facilitate direct energy trading between consumers, reducing the need for intermediaries and improving efficiency.

4. **Carbon Tracking and Sustainability:** Blockchain is used in managing carbon credits and tracing the carbon footprint of generated energy, crucial for addressing climate change.

Examples of Blockchain Applications in the Energy Sector

Blockchain applications in the energy sector are diverse and promising. Some examples include:

- **Microgeneration and Surplus Sale:** Owners of solar energy systems can sell surplus energy directly to other consumers through blockchain.

- **Decentralized Electrical Grids:** Blockchain-based electrical grids allow local energy generation and consumption, reducing losses in distribution.

- **Renewable Energy Tracking Systems:** Renewable energy sources, such as wind and solar, can be transparently and verifiably tracked on the blockchain.

- **Management of Energy Resources:** Smart cities use blockchain for efficient management of energy resources and the reduction of carbon footprints.

Challenges and Considerations

Despite the benefits that blockchain offers in the energy sector and sustainability, there are challenges, such as widespread adoption and the need to address regulatory and interoperability issues between blockchain systems. Additionally, ensuring the privacy and security of data in this area is crucial.

The transformation of the energy sector and the pursuit of sustainability through blockchain are exciting areas promising a cleaner and more sustainable future. As we continue to explore the applications of this technology in other fields, this chapter highlights how blockchain is improving efficiency and transparency in the energy sector, crucial for addressing sustainability challenges and climate change.

Conclusion

Blockchain technology has emerged as a transformative force across a wide range of economic and business fields. Throughout this book, we have explored how blockchain is revolutionizing the way we manage information, conduct transactions, and ensure data integrity in various sectors. From finance to healthcare, from supply chain to intellectual property, blockchain has demonstrated its ability to address critical challenges and provide innovative solutions.

One of the highlights of blockchain is its capacity to enhance transparency. The technology creates immutable and transparent records that enable stakeholders to track and verify the origin of data, assets, and products. This not only increases trust but also reduces the risk of fraud and errors. In a world where information and authenticity are paramount, blockchain emerges as an essential tool.

The automation of processes through smart contracts is another crucial feature of blockchain. These computer programs enable the automatic execution of tasks when specific conditions are met, improving efficiency and reducing reliance on intermediaries. Smart contract applications range from payment management in the supply chain to the automation of copyright management in the creative industry.

Security is a priority in all sectors, and blockchain provides an additional layer of protection. Advanced cryptography and the decentralization of the technology ensure that data and assets are secure and resistant to manipulation. This is especially valuable in areas such as healthcare management and food supply chain security, where data integrity is essential.

However, despite the numerous benefits that blockchain offers, challenges still exist. Widespread adoption of the technology, interoperability between different blockchain systems, and the need to address legal and regulatory issues are areas that require attention. Additionally, it is crucial to ensure the protection of privacy and the management of personal data in blockchain applications.

As we move into the future, it is clear that blockchain will continue to play a fundamental role in the transformation of the economy and business. As obstacles are overcome and more advanced solutions are developed, this technology will continue to bring innovation and improvements in how we handle our data, resources, and assets. From optimizing the supply chain to ensuring the authenticity of intellectual property, blockchain has solidified itself as a driving force defining the economy of the 21st century.